POEMS

DICKHEAD DICKHEAD DICKHEAD DICKHEAD DICKHEAD
DICKHEAD DICKHEAD DICKHEAD DICKHEAD DICKHEAD
DICKHEAD DICKHEAD DICKHEAD DICKHEAD DICKHEAD
DICKHEAD DICKHEAD DICKHEAD DICKHEAD DICKHEAD
DICKHEAD DICKHEAD DICKHEAD DICKHEAD DICKHEAD
DICKHEAD DICKHEAD DICKHEAD DICKHEAD DICKHEAD
DICKHEAD DICKHEAD DICKHEAD DICKHEAD DICKHEAD
DICKHEAD DICKHEAD DICKHEAD DICKHEAD DICKHEAD
DICKHEAD DICKHEAD DICKHEAD DICKHEAD DICKHEAD
DICKHEAD DICKHEAD DICKHEAD DICKHEAD DICKHEAD
DICKHEAD DICKHEAD DICKHEAD DICKHEAD DICKHEAD
DICKHEAD DICKHEAD DICKHEAD DICKHEAD DICKHEAD

DICKHEAD
Wayne F. Burke

DICKHEAD DICKHEAD DICKHEAD DICKHEAD DICKHEAD
DICKHEAD DICKHEAD DICKHEAD DICKHEAD DICKHEAD
DICKHEAD DICKHEAD DICKHEAD DICKHEAD DICKHEAD
DICKHEAD DICKHEAD DICKHEAD DICKHEAD DICKHEAD
DICKHEAD DICKHEAD DICKHEAD DICKHEAD DICKHEAD
DICKHEAD DICKHEAD DICKHEAD DICKHEAD DICKHEAD
DICKHEAD DICKHEAD DICKHEAD DICKHEAD DICKHEAD
DICKHEAD DICKHEAD DICKHEAD DICKHEAD DICKHEAD
DICKHEAD DICKHEAD DICKHEAD DICKHEAD DICKHEAD
DICKHEAD DICKHEAD DICKHEAD DICKHEAD DICKHEAD
DICKHEAD DICKHEAD DICKHEAD DICKHEAD DICKHEAD
DICKHEAD DICKHEAD DICKHEAD DICKHEAD DICKHEAD
DICKHEAD DICKHEAD DICKHEAD DICKHEAD DICKHEAD
DICKHEAD DICKHEAD DICKHEAD DICKHEAD DICKHEAD
DICKHEAD DICKHEAD DICKHEAD DICKHEAD DICKHEAD
DICKHEAD DICKHEAD DICKHEAD DICKHEAD DICKHEAD
DICKHEAD DICKHEAD DICKHEAD DICKHEAD DICKHEAD
DICKHEAD DICKHEAD DICKHEAD DICKHEAD DICKHEAD
DICKHEAD DICKHEAD DICKHEAD DICKHEAD DICKHEAD
DICKHEAD DICKHEAD DICKHEAD DICKHEAD DICKHEAD

BareBackPress

BareBackPress
Hamilton, Ontario, Canada
For enquires visit www.barebackpress.com
For information contact press@barebacklit.com
Cover layout and design by Choi Yunnam

Dedicated to my grandparents:
Edward V. Burke (1902-1964)
Rose T. Burke (1898-1984)

DICKHEAD

a guy on the street
who looks like me:
I clench my fists
in case he tries to
get tough.

Stabbed

I told her while we were
lying in bed:
told her it was over.
She started to weep and
I wanted to comfort her
but could not, would not
and got up and went out
to the kitchen
and poured myself a drink
and she came out of the room
a little later
dry-eyed
and without any clothes on
but not really naked
and said "if I had a knife
when you told me
I'd of stabbed you"
and how glad I was
then
that I had told her in bed
and not in a restaurant.

Ballantine

Whenever I drank Ballantine Ale
I got mean, or
maybe I was already mean;
I don't know;
I don't think so;
but
anyway
one day
not long ago
after emptying several
of the green bottles
I got it into my head
that this big guy
who had an ugly face
I'd seen around town
had somehow
done me wrong
and I saw the guy
on the opposite side of the street
from me
and I screamed
YOU! GET OVER HERE!
like I was talking to a dog
and the guy stared
and I started across the street
and he ran
fast
as I chased him
to a house
he ran inside of
and I followed
up a staircase

to a door
where the guy
stood
holding an axe
and I backed
slowly
down the stairs
and left
just as cops arrived
in their shiny car
that I got a free ride in.

Flaming

The moon is on fire tonight
and the walls of this room
are alive with
rivers flowing
and vegetables growing
and lovely shadows and snow
in black and white like
TV in the 60's
and the radio is on to
a Springsteen song
"can't start a fire"
and I have a fire
in my pants
that can't be extinguished
keeps burning me at night
I get up and jump
into the bathtub
but the fire regenerates
smolders as I sleep
and in the morning
a new scar
I got
to go with
the old one
down the middle
of my heart.

Howl's Cavern

My aunt & uncle pick up
my brother and me
in their car
to take us to Howell's Caverns
in New York State:
I am young
my brother younger
the drive is forever
the walk from where
we park
a hike;
we enter an elevator
dimly lit
lined with chain links
like a cage
and we descend
down
down
down
and I begin to panic
my throat clenched
a scream in my breast
my aunt stands still as a statue
the cage rattles
we reach bottom
get out and walk
as a guide talks
about the difference between
stalactite and stalagmite
and pools of black water
shimmer
ghostly in somber light

and footsteps echo in
the frigid air —
"it is beautiful," says my aunt
but
I do not see it
because
all I can think of
is
going back up
to where
I belong.

Twinkle Twinkle Little Star

I had a bed in my old college roommate's
room
in an apartment rented
by a couple with two kids.
The husband was a stoner and
every night we sat at the kitchen table
and got blasted
until one day it was discovered that
the kids had been molested by
the retired cop who lived next door
and the husband stopped
smoking pot
and got his act together
but I did not
and got kicked out
and slept on park benches
and in the bus station
until
I got a room at the Y—
a closet-sized suite
with a window
and a bed where I could
sleep without worrying
about anything
except the cockroaches
that ran over my face
and woke me;
on clear nights
I'd look through the upper right
window pane
at a star
shining bright

and that star
over many nights
became my star
my beacon
my guiding light
and hope…
but on cloudy nights
without my star
it would only be me
and the roaches
and whatever remained
of the night.

2

you're lion
not lamb,
triumph
not slaughter

Mammals & Reptiles

1.
You sit like a boulder
on the chair
twiddling your thumbs,
leather wing tip shoes on a strut
and Brylcreamed hair shining in
the electric light's hum.
Grandma apologizes for waking us
an hour too soon;
I read my library book THE AGE OF MAMMALS
and wait for the hour hand
on the moon-faced wall clock.
Outside the sky is black as
the La Brea tar pits
where saber-toothed cats
went to feed but met death.

2.
Swirling black and white clouds war
above the ridge line of the mountains.
I climb into the back seat of the car
when we reach Buddy's house
and the overhead light comes on
as Buddy, pumpkin-sized head in
silhouette, says, glancing back,
"who is that, Al?"
I ride in shadow
on vinyl
the engine sound
a lullaby.

3.
The city is a cliff side above;
smell of cigarettes and beer:

people walk in a drizzle as
windshield wipers beat time
to music on the radio.
Yankee Stadium is drenched and dark
as dusk;
a big man in the grandstand catches
a foul ball in his bare hand and
stands like the Statue of Liberty.
Maris hits a bullet into the right field
bleachers
and I wonder who caught it
and how badly it hurt;
I am scared in the public urinal
to take my bibet out and pee
but do;
after the game is rained out
I follow you, broad-shouldered
hippo in the crowd.

4.
At the Bronx Zoo, while you
and Buddy watch a crocodile
eat a rabbit
I hop over to a glass cage
and watch a cobra rise
like a rope and
strike the glass
before my nose...
On the ride home you and Buddy
laugh and smoke
while I sit, invisible
and bored,
staring out the window
and waiting
for the Dawn of Civilization.

Dead Parents

The young female clerk with
the permed hairdo
stops me in the aisle of the 5 & Dime store
and asks
"are you going to pay for the candy?"
"what candy?"
"the candy in your pocket"
"I didn't put any candy in my pocket"
"mind if I look?"
I raise my arms slowly so
the box of JUICY FRUIT
held in the wristband of my coat
does not rattle.
The woman looks confused.
"Come with me," she says
and I follow her to a small dark office
where a store manager sits,
his bald head shaped like a cannonball
nose a beak that could chip through brick;
"we can have the cops come and search you," he says.
I hand the box over.
The woman looks happy.
The manager asks for my mother's phone number.
"My mother is dead," I say.
He asks for my father's number.
"My father is dead."
"Who do you live with?"
"My grandparents."
He looks at the receiver in his hand
then sets it gently into the cradle.
"Get out of here," he says.

Showdown

As I lifted weights in the cellar
I listened to the floor boards overhead
creak
from the weight of my Uncle's feet;
I thought of my fist
landing SPLAT in the middle
of his fat face.
His days as boss man
were past
and he knew it too;
and one morning, in the kitchen
as I combed my hair,
which I had let grow long
he asked when
I was going to get a haircut
and I said "never"
and he flinched
like he'd been slapped
and stared
black-eyed
with the glare that used to
pin me to the floor like a rabbit
but this time I glared back
and we stood
with the sun burning the roof above
and the years piled up between
us;
and then he turned his head
and with a sick smile
fled
out the door
as gutlessly

as every other bully
whoever ran.

Sophomore

Walking down the street
alone
I pass a couple
arm-in-arm and
remember walking with my girl
holding her hand
to the drugstore downtown
for a cherry coke,
careful not to slurp from the straw,
hearing cat-calls from
my buddies on the street
and listening to her chatter
on our way
to the cemetery
where we made-out on
the soft grass, her softer jacket
the tombstones granite
she had to be home by nine
her jacket always stayed
buttoned;
I would have betrayed Christ
for a touch
but
her treasures were locked up
tight:
I dumped her for an older girl
a tease, who dumped me
and then I began to hang out on
the corner, drinking beer
acting tough
one of the boys who
went "over the line"

on weekend nights
to drink
in New York State bars
and drive back
drunk
along snaky roads
passing cars like A.J. Foyt
at Indy.

In Praise Of

The beautiful Shelia O'Ryan
10th grade English teacher
who was from elsewhere
and was flown in with
her long lovely legs dangling
and praised my writing and
read it out-loud to the class;
she was graduated from Bryn Mawr
or Smith, summa cum laude, and
could speak Old English, she said
and did we want to hear some?
Sure we did.
All the guys sat up front
and Schlonski an offensive tackle
kept dropping his pencil to try
and look up her dress
which I hated him for
because to me she was special
like a solar eclipse
and her praise something I needed
something I did not get from anyone else
except coach
who gave it
only if
I knocked someone's head off
onto the field.

Clown

It was a cold day and I was riding the bench
again and
I put on a warm-up jacket
but it was not warm enough so
put on another, then another
six jackets
and I was comfortable
sitting
until the jackass of a coach got the bright idea
in the ninth inning
to have me pinch hit
and I stood and peeled off a jacket,
then another, and another
and heard some snickers
then laughter
and by the sixth jacket hysteria in the stands
and I went up to the plate
and struck-out swinging
on three pitches,
the last one three feet over my head.

Comb

Saturday night at the O. C. Buck Show
we snuck in under the tent flaps
a dozen of us
HURRICANES
red and white football jackets on
and I stood in the front row as
a naked girl stripper with a rosy white body
strutted across the stage
and squatted in front of my face
and I must have blushed
because she said "he's shy,"
and she stood and squatted in front of
Schlonski, an offensive tackle, who
gave the girl his comb
and she combed the hair between her legs
then threw the comb into the air
and it landed at my feet
but I did not
pick it up.

Girlfriend

I met her in the backseat of a car
parked outside a bar
in Hoosic Falls, New York.
She was almost passed-out and
I was about to; in the meantime we did what we could,
which was not much.
I saw her in the hallway in school;
she was a grade ahead of me.
We never spoke.
I never knew her name;
she probably never knew mine.
We kept meeting in back seats; one time
she puked on the car floor
another time we were going good
getting somewhere
when drunks barged in
and ended
whatever
might have been.

3

old friends dead and gone
I salute you
from where I sit:
on the throne
of <u>remimisence</u>

Old Buddy

I stopped in to see my old buddy
in the old neighborhood
and
he did not recognize me
because I wore mirror shades
and I thought he might attack
so tore the glasses off and
then we sat in his backyard which
seemed smaller than I remembered
and when he went back into the house
to get me a beer
his mother came out and
looked at me and said
"I wondered who the bald man in the yard was."
My buddy, who lived in the apartment above
his parents, told me
he was divorced after
his wife ran off with his best friend
and that he, my old buddy, had
got religion
and that
the Bible
was the first book he'd ever read
from beginning to end.

Fruit of the Loom

After having had the shit
kicked out of me
in a bar in Central Square
I walked alone
up the sidewalk bricks
toward Harvard and the Charles River.
The few people I met
gave me
a wide berth
after a gawk at my face
which must not have looked
pretty
and I reached the river bank
and took my pants off
then underwear
which I began to wash out
but thought hell with it and
threw them into the swirling dark
where
they were later found by an oarsman
rowing in a regatta
speared at the end of an oar like a white fish
species unknown.

Railroad Tracks

Hanging out on the railroad tracks
with my buddies,
a hippie ex-ski bum
and a psychiatric patient who
once put a bullet from a thirty-ought-six
into the church steeple.
What am I doing on the tracks, I ask myself.
Wasn't I President of my class in
high school?
Didn't I spend a year at the University?
None of that matters now —
nothing matters except
the pot
and the beer.
Everything else,
like the world situation
for example,
is
like us,
immaterial.

No Daniel Boone

I hiked up to the base of the mountain
while wearing a backpack
and sat
and drank 3 bottles of beer
then hiked to the summit
to live
like a pioneer
and did
for a week
then walked back down
and got a room
in a city strange to me
and did not die
even once
though I passed-out one night
while smoking in bed
and in the morning
discovered
that the cigarette had burnt
a fistula
straight through the mattress.

Madame Judge

The judge, who sat up high
like God,
had a cue-ball white face
and lacquered black bouffant hairdo;
she looked down at the stiffs
from the drunk tank
who filed into the courtroom
like lost sheep
as amateur lawyers argued cases in the hall
and cops stood around with
their arms crossed.
I sat uncomfortably
in a chair
until my name was called
then stood
to face
the Dragon Lady
who said to the prosecuting attorney
"he got off last time — why should we
let him go this time?"
A question that hung in the air
over my head
like a noose.

Eat A Peach

He was a small guy
with glasses and goatee
and the absurd name of
Weimar and
he lived down the hall
in the dormitory and
he wanted, like me, to
write, but unlike me,
he never wrote, or if he
did, never showed it to me.
He introduced me to the
Allman Brothers Band and
to the artistry of W.C. Fields
and whenever we smoked pot
in his room he stuffed a towel
under the door because in
Kansas, in the 70's, pot-smoking
was a felony. His roommate was
a Japanese who would sit cross-
legged on his bed and watch us
smoke and one day I said to him
"fuck you" and he sat bolt upright
looking like a disappointed Kamikaze
and said "rhuck-you!"
I was a funny guy back then but a little
confused and I quit the college after
three months and afterward wrote
Weimar a letter, but he never wrote
back.

The Birds

Feeling lost, as if cast
adrift and
into a gray world,
like a character in an episode of The Twilight Zone,
I leave my room
and walk down the street
to the park
and lean against the granite base
of a lamp post,
sky darkening with dusk,
and a bird flies down
and lands by my hand
and I reach a finger and stroke
its breast
and when it flies off
another lands
and I pat its head
and stroke its feathers;
and a girl, walking past
slows to gawk
but
then the bird flies off
and so too does the girl.

The Wake

Two of my nephews
dressed in dark suits
like Mafia guys
sprawl in chairs
looking like convicts
awaiting execution
on either side of my sister
who has circles under her eyes
like the mud flaps on trucks.
Nearby, my Aunt sits
smiling,
happy because the nephew in the casket
is going to get to meet Jesus...
I kneel by the body
which looks poured into the box —
the way they always look —
and I choke back a sob
or it chokes itself
and then I stand
and look
for a place to sit
but
there isn't one.

A Winner

Driving home from work at midnight
down the belt-line
doing seventy in my Altima Thule XL
in a ridiculously posted
50 mph zone
a car far behind
comes on strong
maybe a cop
and I slow to sixty
and the car
an old sedan
slides past
some peckerwood at the wheel
and I speed up
and we head
neck and neck
down a dog leg
to a hare-pin turn
and the hot shot pulls in front
and when his brake lights go on
I cut into the left lane
and pass him on the turn
as he almost wipes out
as I blow through
the green light,
yhay
I've won!
Won what?
Won nothing—
could have caused a fiery crash—
why'd I do it?
Must have needed to win

at something.

Les Perdu

I am lying on the beach
no one else around
when a little girl appears
tears rolling down her cheeks;
"pourquoi?" I ask
and she replies in French.
I search for words to answer.
We have a conversation
of sorts.
"Vous parlez Anglais?"
No, she does not.
"Ou votre parents?"
"Je ne sais pas."
Lost her parents
and is at a hotel
but does not know which.
Name is Nicolette.
Takes 5 minutes to get this out,
my tongue fumbling for words.
I spot two guys and a woman
walking past and
call "monsieurs! Madame!
Un moment!"
They come right over,
quiz the girl.
"Thanks," one of the Frogs says
in English,
"we'll take it from here."

4

a car stops
in the street
woman in the passenger seat
asks me "are you loco?"
"yes, I am," I say

Seat 27·B

We are at twenty-seven thousand feet
there is an old lady on my right
she is chewing and fidgeting
maybe saying her prayers
she becomes self-conscious when I look
across her to see out the window
on my left is an asshole
with a suit on, Mr. Spick and Span
he looks like the MC on JEOPARDY
he is invisible, does not want to be
touched or looked at or acknowledged
he reads a New York Times
he has taken possession of the armrest
I am in the middle
stuck
without a newspaper
or a prayer.

East to Cornstalk

The beer cans pile up around me
on the seat as
the train heads east;
I ask every girl who passes in the aisle
if she'd like a drink;
one sits and does
one sits and doesn't
and the conductor, who said in Cheyenne
he'd seat a "pretty girl" beside me,
but never did — gives me dirty looks.
The teetotaler chick is going somewhere
in the corn fields; she is impressed by me
I can tell...
I lose her though
and in a fevered dream
as Chicago looms
my eyes slide shut like the sun sinking
below the horizon.
When I wake I take a room
with red velvet drapes
and feel like King Shit
until morning
when I tug on my new silken
J C Penny shirt
and lug my suitcase and hangover
back to the station.

Flight 2014

Squashed into a window seat
my face in the porthole
looks back at me;
there is a wing out there
somewhere
and a city of dazzling lights
below
and a coastline
and ocean beyond where
the lights don't shine…
the stewardess dangles a mask
in her hands
with what looks like a giant condom attached
and my dick rubs against my pants
and the engines throb
and the big jet shudders
and I fly through the dark
ready to sleep or fuck
or
whatever.

Goodbye Deidre and Patrick

I got disgusted because
no one would give me a
ride, and I said "the hell
with them — I will walk"
and I walked until I came
to a pub outside of Wexford
and I went inside and drank
with the people, and told
them I was going to walk
around Ireland and some
wished me luck and one
grave-faced guy took me
aside to warn me of the
dangers, especially in the
north-west, and I thanked
him and the others and
bought 3 warm bottles of
stout for myself and went
and walked until the road
was black as tar and my
feet had disappeared, and
then a car came along
and Deidre and Patrick from
the pub took me to their
home and gave me a cot
and I slept until morning
when I woke and left
without saying goodbye.

A Lark Up the Nose of Time

We left Kansas after
the bars closed
Ron and Steve and me
in a station wagon
that I passed-out
in the back of
and woke
below a huge steel arch
high above
like a gate to heaven,
but it was Saint Louis
which we bombed through
all the way to Daytona
and got a hotel room
and sat indoors for three days
as
hurricane winds drove white sea horses
to shore and
branches of palm trees whirled
like broken helicopter blades...
On day four we got sun burnt
and drunk
and I was so hungry
that night
I punched out the Plexi-glass
of a candy machine
and tried to eat a candy bar
old as World War One
and in the morning I woke
wet
from piss
in my bed

and
covered the spot
and we drove back
out of money
out of smokes
and Ron got ugly
without his fix
and Steve
a born-again liar
told one whopper after
another
all the way to Ottawa.

The Faamer

A farmer who looks a lot like
Georgie Jessel the comedian,
same graying brush-cut hair,
glasses — he and I are on our
way to Middlebury, Vermont
in his pickup, and as he drives
he talks about farming stuff
and as he talks his right hand
creeps across the seat toward
my leg. Just my luck, I think
to be picked-up by a farming
closet queer, but I need the ride
and talk to the guy while I watch
the hand get closer then retreat
and start the trek over, and I wonder
if I'll have to break his finger or
maybe jaw but then the sign for
Middlebury appears and I say
"pull over" and the old weirdo
stops the truck.

Hot Dog

I returned to New York
from Ireland
with no money
and sat for two days
in the LaGuardia Airport lobby
waiting for a 25$ money order
through Western Union.
A church group from Kansas
sat down around me and
I debated religion with
a minister who preached to me on Christian
charity and
I put him to the test
when I hit him up for
change
which he gave,
enough for a hot dog,
which I ate
with relish
as the minister's wife
gave me a fish-eyed appraisal.

no work today
except on my tan
and writing
this
immortal tanka

Truck Driver

Stepped out of the ditch
and let go of the shovel
and took hold of the wheel
of a dump truck
that I had trouble backing up
and went off the road twice
stopping the job each time as they towed me out
and the supervisor
after the second time
said "get out of the truck"
and I climbed down
but did not take the shovel
he offered
because
I had calluses enough.

Doughnuts

I got off work at 3 in the morning
after working another twelve hour shift
and I drove my car
to the P & C Market
where I turned a few doughnuts
on the ice
before I parked and
got out
and walked to the door
where some guy,
who stood looking at me,
said "I don't care how old you are,
don't pull doughnuts in the lot"
and I said
"FUCK YOU"
and he blinked behind
his cock-eyed glasses
and I followed him inside
and asked if he'd heard
what I said,
but he did not reply
and I went about my shopping
too tired to
give a shit
or
take any
either.

Whack-A-Nut

I was guard for
Whack-A-Nut security
and got assigned
to an empty factory
and brought books, a typewriter,
and radio to work
and sat
in a corner
and smoked weed if I had any
and hoped no one would break in
and bother me.
Stan, my relief, came in early
one night and said he'd seen a guy
on the roof and
said we should go up and
get the son-of-a-bitch
and I asked Stan what he would do if
he caught the guy
and Stan said "if he's my size
I'll beat the shit out of him."
Stan wasn't very big,
and I refused to go
to the roof with him.

Another night, I locked myself out
of the building and
had to break a window with a stone
to get back in
and foolishly threw the rock
back out
and when no rock was found inside
I was questioned

and laid down a line of shit
to keep the job
but two weeks later
was fired
when the supervisor
found me with my feet up reading
a book and smoking a joint
as the radio played smooth jazz.

A Man's Work

The clerk at the store said
"pickin' oranges be a man's work."
Had to rip the little buggers from
the tree—like the State taking kids
out of a home—and the branches
full of thorns, and the sweat pouring,
enough to water lawns, and the farmer
a good ole boy racist atop his tractor
watching us bleed and sweat.

Tied a noose onto a pole to tug the
topmost oranges off, wore long-sleeved
shirts, laid a sheet to catch the yellow balls
that fell in staccato bursts. A 3 by 5 foot
bin 5 bucks worth. The farmer began to
talk-up his daughter to us; Jamaicans in the
next row out-picked us though: almond eyes,
coffee-colored skin, they would not stop to chat.

The bins filled slower than a baseball game;
we got bored, ran out of talk, quit; had to
boss each other: say "get to work you son-
of-a-bitch!" Say "how about you, you ain't
done shit!" Like that. Cooled off at the
swimming hole which was no Myrtle Beach
but cold enough and wet. Listened to them
bugs screech: WEEP WEEP WEEP! Regular
as breath. Pocketed our money and headed
for the coast and the Land of Milk and Honey
only we never made it, and probably never will.

The Fruit Market

I got sent to work
at the Fruit Market
on the Chelsea-Everett line
outside Boston
where I sat in a shack
and checked-in trucks
entering and leaving.

I wore a sky blue cop uniform.

Before work one day
I stopped in the hotel-bar
across the street from the market
for a quick one
and realized,
after I entered
that everyone in the joint had suddenly
become quiet
and I drank my beer quickly
and left.

During the shift a truck driver
and his wife
came up to the shack window
and he told me they were from
Nebraska
and that they had gone into the hotel-bar
across the street
looking for a room to rent.

An old guy wearing a soiled fedora
and a self-effacing woman

cut out of a Grant Wood picture.

"I didn't think they let things like that
go on in Boston," he said.

"Things like what?"

He nodded to the hotel-bar.
"That place is a whorehouse!"

I lost that job soon
afterward
because
while putting up the American flag
on the pole behind the shack
I unthinkingly let the flag touch the ground
and the boss man—
a red-faced prick who looked like he had not
shit in a month—
fired me.

6

6 o'clock is
no excuse to go off
and get yourself
annihilated
by the Mongols

Unwell Beach

Sun setting on Wells Beach,
Maine.
I don't think I've liked anyone
today:
argued with a woman
over a beach chair,
argued with a salesgirl
over price of a sale;
a slender blonde next door
speaking French to her
long-haired boyfriend,
hotel on a street
full of telephone poles
and lines
connecting somewhere.

Awake

I guess I am supposed to be
awake tonight
and staring into the darkness behind
my eyelids
and thinking of what I'll buy tomorrow
at the market;
I guess I am meant to be
in the dark and
review my history,
think of what I've read
and seen,
or not think —
rub my head on the bedpost
and then,
finally, dream
and wake
to know I'd slept.

Gods

The gods will come through
for me
like the sea to shore
my life will flame,
the moon will blaze for me
once more
the crickets will cheer me like the hero
of the game
I'll walk on flowers
down honied pathways beside
crystal waters
King for a day
or an hour the hours the sunflowers bow
and crows call my name
and rivers gurgle my praise
oh gods
you have come through
like the sun to horizon.

Stress

Woke
feeling stressed
8 A.M.
bedroom overcast
the telephone blinking
with a call from work
asking for more hours of
my life
plus a dream
in my head
of me escorting a woman
two girls, two cats
through busy city streets —
a job and a half
and I'm beat
and have not even
brushed my teeth
yet.

4 A.M.

I turn on the light and
pick up my pencil
to write
as I lie alone
in bed
a lump of flesh and bone
my back to the mattress
below a cold moon
and dim stars
that look down
on the dying
in their beds
and the dead
lying still as stone
on earth
where
the worms
have won.

Escape

It almost hits me
the black sedan
coming down the hill
and as
I watch the car,
sleek and somehow
sinister,
I get ready to run
into the woods
should the car
turn around,
but it doesn't turn
and I continue
up the street
which is now a river
and I'm in to my ankles
moving stealthily
like an escapee from prison
trying to throw the dogs
off my scent.

Wake-up

I just woke
from a nap,
an hour in
an afternoon
dark with clouds
and rain:
get up, I told myself
there is much to do
like read all
of Proust
or visit Niagara Falls
and eat
and drink
and look out the window
at the sky
opening to immensities
of space
beyond the dark
and dismal-seeming day
which is
in a way
quite beautifully
somber:
pitched in gray,
charcoal,
smoke,
white slather of clouds
and sheen of rain
on metal roof
seen from the
window of this
a.p.t.

Up & Out

Awoke at 3 A.M.
again
and got up
and sat in the dark
of the kitchen
until a wall began to look
like an Arshile Gorky painting
then I returned to bed
and tried to pray myself
to sleep
but could not do it
so lay
listening to the universe
which
does not speak
and then
I woke
10 A.M.
and quickly got up
because
the sun
the sun
was up.

Bread & Water

You want me live
on bread and water
but I can't;
I've tried,
it's a killer;
I turn resentful
then bitter
start to compare
myself to others
ask why
they have
and me without—
would you tell me that?
No, of course not
because you don't speak;
okay, so don't--
just throw me a scrap
once in awhile
something to chew on
that tastes better
than hemlock.

Smiler

The young nurse comes in
smiling
like she never had a
problem
or a pain
and I look up at her pearly whites
and want to take a rag
and wipe the smile off her face
and as she speaks
I try not to look at her
or listen
and finally
she beams herself
elsewhere.

Deep Freeze

Brown and yellow leaves
swamp the ground for
miles around
4 feet deep
children are lost
and never found
until Spring
thaw
when whole families
appear
frozen solid
not seen since
autumn
when the snow started
and the woolly mammoths began
to migrate
south
instead of hanging around the
Freeze Your Ass Off State.

Monday Morning

I leave the a.p.t. and go to the diner;
a male waiter,
but OK;
I read the newspapers;
same characters on the streets as yesterday,
same places to avoid;
two homeless in the park argue
as jets fill the blue sky with
streaming white vapor trails
and Gomer with a cigarette
sits beside me,
talks about the weather
and asks questions about my job
which
I do not answer
because
I will be there
soon enough.

Blue lights

A sign on the roadside
read STAY ALERT
and I thought
better slow down
but
I was going downhill
and decided I'd slow
on the upswing
and went flying
past a State Trooper
his car
like a crouching panther
in the weeds
and I said god no
shit
balls
piss
damn
and slowed to a crawl
but the cop came after me
blue lights flashing
and I pulled over
fully ALERT.

Birdies

Blue and white chickadees the size of
my thumb
and a small cardinal with
black Quaker beard around its beak
plus tiny brown sparrows
in the apple tree below
the porch
where I stand in
dull November light
below a bird house I found
and hung
but none have moved in yet
because
maybe too close
for those
who do not know
that
I am harmless
unless provoked.

turkeys on the run
from hunters with
guns—
the mashed potatoes
balk
at being lumped with
the squash
and the cranberry sauce
laments the loss
of table space
to stuffing up
the orifice
of the state bird

Visitors

There is a flying saucer
hovering
a big mother
from the Planet Crouton
in galaxy X-10
and with gamma ray guns
enough to destroy the city
but for some reason
they don't
and when a rope is thrown
from the craft
a little man
climbs down
to the street
and goes inside of Dunkin' Donuts
and asks for the restroom key
which they won't give
because he is not
a paying customer.

Alone

He lived in a back room
of DD's Bar & Grill.
His name was Pete
or Art or Earl
and he had come to town
from somewhere else
long ago.
Aloneness clung to him
like a coat;
alone in a crowd
alone in the street
alone smoking a cigarette
that he cupped in the palm of his hand—
his face was a mask
hammered from stone
and DD rode his ass
if he, Earl or Art or
Pete, did not sweep or
mop fast enough
or clean the glasses
until they shone.

From Brooklyn He Is

Fred wears tinted glasses
and used to be a speed freak
when he drove truck for Pepsi-Cola
but he got diabetes
and had his legs cut off
below the knees
and one day I see him
walking
down the sidewalk
only instead of six-two
he's five-eight
with two plastic stumps
for legs
and a cane in each hand
and the stumps
clunk clunk
on the cement
and he's sweating like a waterfall
because it's hot
and because he can barely stand
but when the bus pulls to the curb
he hikes the steps
like Hillary making the ascent
of Everest
and he waves from behind the tinted glass.

Dogs

He owed me a shit-load of money
for the dope
but would not pay up
so
one day I climbed the hill
across the street from his house
and lay in the grass
waiting
until the fuck came out
and then I rested the stock
of my thirty-ought-six
on my shoulder
and sited the cross-hairs
and shot
the dog
and that guy
you should have seen him
run—
like a jackrabbit—
and afterward
he started to cough up
a few bucks
and I was glad
though
I did feel bad
for that dog.

Daddy

My daddy lined us up
smallest to biggest
eight kids
like a set of stairs
and he gave each of us
a glass
according to our size—
the babies got shot glasses—
and daddy filled
the glasses with gin
and when he said so
we all drank
and we drank every night
for years
and four of my brothers
a sister, and me
became alcoholics
like daddy
who had a hemorrhage one day
and went to the hospital
where he could not drink
but I smuggled in a bottle
and stood by his bed
and watched him drink every drop
and the next day
he died
the bastard.

Imperator

After I became emperor
I had a couple hundred
dirty so-and-so's
hung on crosses
outside my office
and each morning after
breakfast I'd walk
beneath them and
tickle their feet with a feather
and some would curse,
call me a bastard
but
I tell you
it did me good
to see them squirm
of course
I could have had them cut down
and boiled them in oil
but crucifixion was
more enjoyable for me
personally
because I got to torment them
longer
like the one who kept
calling
"Abba Abba"
(and I'd reply "abba-abba-do!")
a long haired dirty hippie type
convicted of selling Pablum to children;
I couldn't stand him
but
I have to hand it
to him
because

unlike the others
he never once
called me
a bastard.

Prayer

I prayed to god but
no help came
so I prayed to the Virgin Mary
and she came to my room
one night
and asked what did I want
and I said
"a woman"
and she said
that
she was sorry but
she was a virgin and
determined to stay one
and why didn't I take
my next vacation
in Nevada
where I could go to a house
and legally buy
whatever I wanted?
and I told the Virgin
thanks
for the suggestion
but
I'd already done that
once
and never would again.

Drronk

He went on a drunk
and talked everyone's ears
off—
a guy who says two words
a week;
he's sleeping on a park bench now
dead to the world
and dreaming of
flying saucers landing
and little gray men
with obsidian eyes
holding his hand
and bringing him aboard
while talking non-stop
in a language
he cannot understand.

Vote For Shitmore

I ran for Congress
on the flat platform
the wooden one,
and promised everything
to everyone
and got elected
but did not do a damn thing
because
between Republican and Democrat
we're frozen solid
nothing I could get done,
nobody can,
and everyone knows
we're going over the falls
in a barrel
but
it looks like fun
to them
but it won't be
when the splatter comes
but
you tell 'em that
I won't
I got promises to make
and more to break
too.

Fright Night

We soaped windows
and smashed some pumpkins
then we rolled some logs
out onto the highway
that caused a major accident
in which two people died
then we set a house on fire
and shot the residents with a .22
as they ran out
and hung their bodies up
in an apple grove
we chopped down
and used as kindling for
a bonfire we roasted a couple family pets
over
plus two handicapped people we
kidnapped from the home...
It was a lot of fun
a blast
but the night was still young
so we chartered a boat
and sailed out into the ocean
and stabbed whales to death
with a pitchfork
plus dumped a ton of oil into the water
and cut-up the fish that died
and spread their guts
on the highway
and watched accidents happen
as we relaxed
knowing
that
even if caught
we'd get off with a slap

because
hey
everyone is entitled to some fun
on Halloween.

Hard-Boiled

I handed the clerk my
note
but the dumb bitch
could not read my writing
and looked at me as if
I had two heads
or was green
and when I told her "hurry up"
she acted like she was waiting for the bus
so
I shot her
and then I shot the manager
who came running out of the office
like a hero
and he died on the floor over by
the pretzels
and I got out of there
thinking that
they both died for a hundred bucks
which was chicken shit
but that clerk
she should have been able to read
better
and that manager
he was just
a jerk.

Monkey's Uncle

They played classical music
to calm the apes
who were intent
upon rape and
mayhem until
they heard Brahms,
then they sat back
and put on the
tuxedoes the women
gave them to wear
and the apes went
to the ball smelling
like perfumed frauds
with their hair combed
back and during the
Concerto in E-Minor
sat rapt and only
scratched themselves
during intermission.

good as winning the lottery
without having bought
a ticket;
good as watching
Ali vs: Frazier
or Army vs: Navy;
good as reading the
poetry of
Peter Jelen;
good as a Cadillac's
engine;
good as having my cock
squeezed by
Miss America.

Buk

Arthur Hoyle writes
that
my poetry reminds him
of Bukowski
which I take as compliment
though not knowing
if Arthur meant it as such—
Bukowski the truth-say-er
comedy-maker
crafty
sly
honest
liar
who
drilled his words
onto paper
in a hurry
in a race
like the rest of us
against
big daddy Death.

Don Corleone

She starts telling me
about her ex-boyfriend;
that he is a nice guy
and fun to be with
and that he knows everyone...
and that he is in the Mafia.

The Mafia?

"Yea," she says, smiling
"you know—like 'The Godfather.'"

I lock the apartment door,
pull the shades,
and unplug the telephone.

"And does he know that
you're here—with me?"

"No. He's looking for me
in Boston."

I peek out a window;
the street is dark and empty;
someone could be lurking
unseen in the shadows:
someone like Sonny Corleone.

"You're so paranoid," she says,
still with the smile, like something—
I can't imagine what—is funny.

I turn the lamp down and think about
Barricading the windows with mattresses.

Are those footsteps I hear?
Or the beating of my heart?

Vaseline

It was her suggestion
and I said "go get it"
and she got out of bed
and her feet
pat pat pat
to the bathroom and back
and I took the jar from her hand
and spread some goo on her
as she waited, on all fours
patient as a dog
and then I got it inside of her
past the sphincter
and into air:
like fucking a balloon
but she liked it
maybe because
it was how her mother took it
from the old man
who beat her first
and always said
afterward
"she's got an ass that just won't quit."

Dickhead

Sitting in the park
after dark
with my cock out
like a little telescope
looking for submarines—
the park is surrounded with
spotlights and
maybe a few cameras...
I wonder if the vice-squad will arrive:

"ALRIGHT BUDDY! What you got there?"

Badges flash:

"Dick out in the park! That's a five-oh-seven! Book him!"

My cock starts to shrink,
retreats like a mole into its hole.

I squint at names of Civil War dead on a plaque.

My cock suddenly stands and salutes:
"suck me suck me," it says.

"Pipe down!" I say
"do you want to get us arrested?"

"Eat shit," my cock says,
"and also—keep your goddamn hands off me."

I zip up.

"I'll try," I say
"but no guarantees."

Mrs. Baguette

Light peeks over the ridge line
of mountains like a slice of window
in the night
and Mrs. Baguette reaches back,
undoes her bra strap,
and her tits fall like baseballs
onto her stomach.

Charlie Baguette comes around the corner
of the house, his fists balled.
"HEY! WHAT ARE YOU LOOKIN' AT?"

"What do you think
dumb shit!
Your Ma's tits!
I think I'll go in
and fuck her!"

"NO YOU WON'T!
I'LL KILL YAH!"

"NO YOU WON'T!
I'LL KILL YOU!"

"I'll get my father's gun!"

"I'll get my grandmother's butcher knife!"

"TRY! And see what happens!

"I WILL! Don't worry!"

"I AIN'T WORRIED!"

"I AIN'T EITHER! So there!"

"SO THERE yourself!"

Charlie goes into the house.
His mom has a pink teddie on
that glows; she winks at me
from the window; I think I WILL
go in and fuck her.

Doc Morrison

"Mr. Burke, the doctor will see you now."

The receptionist holds the door open;
she has a set of big jugs and
I try and give her an elbow shot as I walk past
but she dodges it.

"Hello, Doc."

The Doc has an uncanny resemblance to the late
Jim Morrison of THE DOORS.

"How you feeling, m'boy?"

"Awful. My neck hurts. My back is sore. I can barely
get out of bed in the morning. I think I got rheumatoid
arthritis or somethin'..."

"Well, at our age we have to expect some pain."

"SOME pain, yea, but Christ, I'm dying."

"I wouldn't worry about it if I were you."

"You're not me."

"Ha ha. That's true." He opens a desk drawer and
shows me two handfuls of pill bottles. "What do you
want to take?" He spreads the bottles on the desk.
"These are good...These here will fix you in a hurry...
These I take myself—even when I don't have pain, ha
ha!"

"You're a character, Doc."

"Yes, I know. Everyone calls me Doctor Feel Good;
except the women, they call me Doctor Feel-You-Up...

You should have seen the one I had in here last week—"
He stretches his arms out, hands turned inward: "she
had 'em out to here..."

"I don't like taking pills."

"No? What do you want, an operation? I'll set you up
with Dumore in Rheumatology." He makes a note on
the
desk blotter.

"Thanks Doc."

"Don't mention it."

He ushers me to the door.

"How about that receptionist?" I ask.

"Her? You can try if you want; I tapped
her a couple of times...Won't give head
though; against her religion, or something."

"Well Doc, keep it up, ha ha."

"I will. I think it's coming up now. Mr. Mojo
rising!"

"A rider on the storm!"

"On more than the storm, ha ha!"

"The LA woman!"

"Right! Minneapolis too!"

"Ha ha! So long Doc!"

"So long!"

The receptionist smiles as I approach.

She is ready to light my fire.

Acknowledgements:

I would like to thank the following publications, where some of the poems used in this book first appeared: Lost Coast Review, Fish Food Magazine, Tipsy Lit, The Screech Owl, the bicycle review, Bareback Magazine, Contraposition, The Commonline Journal, Brickplight, Phantom Kangaroo, Insert, Ricochet, American Tanka, Dead Flowers, Crack the Spine, Manic Fervor, Locust, Dirty Chai, and Industry Night.

Author's Note:

Not once as a kid growing up in a small mill-town in the hills of North Berkshire County, Massachusetts, did I think of becoming a poet. I wanted to become a Major League baseball player, and if I could have hit a curve-ball with more facility than I showed, I might have become one. Or maybe not: I had a lot of other things beside baseball on my mind in adolescence. Not poetry through. Only in college did poetry show up, for me, on the radar screen. My college roommate, a tough guy from a similar background as mine, and also an ex-jock like me, not only wrote poetry but read what he wrote to whomever would listen. He was beautiful; militant in his advocacy of poetry, and because of his example I began my first attempts to write a poem. I was nineteen at the time and at my second college and destined to attend two more before awarded a "Bachelor of Arts" degree quantifying me a totally worthless entity to the business and commercial world. A world I remained on the periphery of and low-down on the food chain for a number of years—years during which I thought more about writing poetry than actually writing any. Years in which the idea of being a poet was more enticing to me—and far easier—than doing the work involved in becoming a poet (or even a facsimile thereof). At some point in my later 30's—the exact chronology is beyond me—I published a few poems, but poetry was a sort of sideline to me; prose was what I worked at. Rather than poet, I considered myself scholar, critic, and novelist of the future. That I was 3rd rate as scholar, 2nd rate as critic, and un-rated as novelist, did not deter me. I published two books of literary criticism in my 40's, and had numerous book reviews, articles, and some short stories published during my 50's...And then I gave up. Quit. Stopped writing and concentrated on drawing pictures; also went to nursing school and became licensed as an LPN. And then I had a heart attack. Or what I thought a heart attack, later diagnosed as arterial heart disease. Serendipitously, as I see it, I had begun writing again, strictly poetry, just previous to my diagnoses, and after by-pass surgery (triple though I was shooting for quintuple) I began writing daily and with a sort of vengeance. A schedule I have followed these past two years and one that has resulted in the book you hold in your hand as well as a previously published volume (WORDS THAT BURN) and at least one future volume (now in larval stage). The writing has been a lot of work and a lot of fun too and I plan for more of both, so...stay tuned.

Wayne F. Burke

Also by the Author

Words That Burn

BEWARE: Wayne F. Burke and his Words that Burn is not only poetry, its arson. A combustible collection of poetry that will fry anyone's imagination: jails, arrests, a bad childhood, and life in the raw. Words that Burn is a brutally honest evisceration of one man's experience of life on this planet written with verve and the unadorned yet eloquent language of where the poet came from.

$12.00
132 pages
6 x 9
ISBN-13: 978-0992035518
ISBN-10: 0992035511
BISAC: Poetry / General
BareBackPress

Praise for Words That Burn

"One of the most unapologetically honest books I have read...A poet who takes no prisoners, pulls no punches, wastes no words and knows how to tell a good story...Burke not only has the guts to admit his part in the fractured society he makes comment on, he also has the audacity to make art out of it...A sane voice in a mad world."

~ Matthew J. Hall,
Screaming With Brevity

"...the brutal evisceration of one man's experience of life on the planet earth. Burke writes with confidence, and swag...unforgettable imagery, black humor...something in these experiences that everyone can, or will, relate to."

~ Peter Jelen, author of
Impressions Of An Expatriate

"Burke is a tough young poet who, like all the rest of us, has learned some lessons from William Carlos Williams, but without imitating Williams. Burke writes the language of where he came from and with respect for it, and more power to him."

~ Alan Dugan, author of
Collected Poems,
Winner of The National Book Award
and the Prix de Rome.

BareBackPress

www.barebackpress.com